THE AMERICAN POETRY REVIEW/HONICKMAN
FIRST BOOK PRIZE

The Honickman Foundation is dedicated to the support of projects that promote spiritual growth and creativity, education and social change. At the heart of the mission of the Honickman Foundation is the belief that creativity enriches contemporary society because the arts are powerful tools for enlightenment, equity and empowerment, and must be encouraged to effect social change as well as personal growth. A current focus is on the particular power of photography and poetry to reflect and interpret reality, and, hence, to illuminate all that is true.

The annual American Poetry Review/Honickman First Book Prize offers publication of a book of poems, a $3,000 award, and distribution by Copper Canyon Press through Consortium. Each year a distinguished poet is chosen to judge the prize and write an introduction to the winning book. The purpose of the prize is to encourage excellence in poetry, and to provide a wide readership for a deserving first book of poems. *Rough Honey* is the thirteenth book in the series.

WINNERS OF THE AMERICAN POETRY REVIEW/HONICKMAN
FIRST BOOK PRIZE

ROUGH HONEY

WINNER OF THE APR/HONICKMAN FIRST BOOK PRIZE

ROUGH HONEY

MELISSA STEIN

The American Poetry Review

Philadelphia

Cover photograph: Arielynn Cheng

Distribution by Copper Canyon Press/Consortium.

Library of Congress Control Number:

ISBN 978-0-9776395-5-7 (cloth, alk. paper)
ISBN 978-0-9776395-9-5 (pbk., alk. paper)

FIRST EDITION

for the we of me

Contents

Introduction

"If we were / made to be whole," Melissa Stein suggests, in the first poem in this vital and various book,

> we wouldn't be so lost
> to each offering of tenderness and a story.

But her readers can't know just how seriously she means this proposition against coherence until they arrive at the book's second poem, which presents us with lines such as:

> ... it was a blast, meeting it all cranium-first,
> like academics, frothfoamgrit and the taste,
> what was it, asphyxiation, psychedelic Escher
> in blackwhite cubes, tableau enormous, picnic
> tablecloth but undulating, spiked into color—crimson,
>> canary—

or

> what a party, annihilation, till the blue blue blue

There's something thrilling about moving rapidly from the tight choreography of punctuated sentences to a rush of language that "sentences" in an entirely different way. This formal signal underscores that first poem's premise: that to be "whole" is to be artificially coherent, and to be partial is to be open to—well, practically everything.

This openness—of form, and of the receptive and longing body— is *Rough Honey*'s central subject, and its oxymoronic title suggests the sweet and fierce character of desire, that compelling and dangerous sustenance. Clearly those wild rapids that flip the speaker's boat in "Whitewater" are also the heady current of eros:

and the ache of return, to the tenderness
of paint sable-brushed against silk, powdered
throat of the foxglove, flushed curve spiraling
into a conch, velvet crowning the doe's nose,
arms embracing the cello's hips, shoulders . . .

Those lines feel like a kind of seizure of longing, a sexual charge spreading out from the speaker into the perceived world, not unlike the sort of vision granted to the poet in section five of "Song of Myself," when, in the afterglow of sex, Whitman's speaker notices that

. . . limitless are leaves stiff or drooping in the fields,
And brown ants in the little wells beneath them,
And mossy scabs of the worm fence, heap'd stones, elder,
    mullein and poke-weed.

Except, of course, that the visionary has been filled with "peace and knowledge," whereas the ruptures and breakages of the self that fill *Rough Honey* seem to bring anything but. It is impossible, in the terms of Stein's world, not to admit others; even the neighbors' voices (*"I told you never to fuck you just fuck you you fucking fuck"*) can't be held at bay. But the incompleteness of the individual self means that we're always subject to danger, and therefore *Rough Honey* fills up with speakers in many kinds of trouble: rapists, murderers, a butcher's daughter drawn to knives, women harmed by their lovers, a girl sold into marriage by a dangerous father, a woman in danger from a stranger in a passing car on a country road. Melissa Stein does indeed contain multitudes, all linked by the way that desire's sweetness doesn't seem to be separable from trouble, and how we can neither set down that quest for that sugar nor embrace it without complication.

Stein's poems are lit by a restless and flashing verbal intelligence. She's marvelously attentive to the world ("the cows are free / under their corsets of flies, / breaking and entering / chlorophyll"), and she has an effortless way of moving from the particular to the general:

> . . . we don't even know
> where we put the keys last night,
> or why no beauty's loud enough
> to drown out rage and drown out sorrow.

Her sentences are beautifully choreographed; they start and stop the motion of her poems with a nearly invisible, effortless authority. Best of all, her concurrent attention to sound and to image makes the world, on these pages, viscerally real; she employs one of poetry's oldest powers, yoking the referentiality of words to their sheer sonic force, and thus forging a spell that refreshes the reader's perception, convincing us of the fleshy actuality of what's placed before us:

> Holding a hare by the ears
> he tugs the skin off the meat,
> relishing the *shhhh* of the fascia.
> What's under the fur is a secret.
> What's under the skin is divine.

Of late many a young poet has chosen a controlling project for a first book. I'm making these examples up, but consider, for example, forty poems in the voice of Sacajawea, or a volume centered on the history of tattooing, or one using a formal pattern, say sonnet variations, to establish coherence. There are two advantages to doing so: the poet gains leverage for the making of more poems, as the project begins to establish a direction and suggest new work. And the book can be readily described, both by poet and publisher. It is difficult to describe poetry well, and one may be grateful for a simple, coherent plan that can be stated in a few words.

But there can be a cost to such predetermination, too; it's often those messy or rebellious elements that seem to spill out of a design, that won't conform to a standard, that make poetry strangely and rewardingly alive. Maybe my discomfort with this arises because I myself seem incapable of corralling my poems in this way; as soon as I decide to make a book of short lyrics, or to develop a long sequence attending to animal lives, my imagination seems to insist on doing something else. I admire inclusiveness, the whole that only gradually reveals itself, the garden that can't really be apprehended till you've walked all the way around and tried to assemble a vision of the entirety. Coherence has its virtues, but perhaps a market economy in which a plethora of poets strives to be noticed tends to overvalue them. Might we replace a desire for consistency with a healthy variety of interests, both in terms of content and of form? Perhaps, out of such variety, principles of unity emerge which are subtler and more complex than those consciously chosen. Wholeness—whatever it is our art can have of that quality—seems more trustworthy when it *emerges.*

Melissa Stein is a formal polymath. Elegant sonnets, more-or-less-narrative free verse, short aphoristic lyrics, unpunctuated cascades of anaphora, a poem made primarily of what appears at first to be nonsense and then reveals itself as a catalog of words for wind, dramatic monologues, a pantoum, elliptical sequences—she seeks out whatever she can use for the needs of a particular poem, and makes of all that a multifaceted examination of longing: rough ardor, tough honey, dangerous sweetness.

Mark Doty

ROUGH HONEY

Olives, Bread, Honey, and Salt

The lanes are littered with the bodies of bees.
A torrent took them, swarming in branches
just as the white buds loosened their hearts
of pale yellow powder. Each body is a lover:
the one with skin blank as pages; the one
so moved by the pulse ticking in your throat;
the one who took your lips in his teeth
and wouldn't let go; the one who turned
from you and lay there like a carcass. If we were
made to be whole, we wouldn't be so lost
to each offering of tenderness and a story.
Therefore our greatest longing is our home.
There is always the one bee that circles and circles,
twitching its sodden wings.

Whitewater

kayak flipped us and the current
dragged us through its rocks, arms sealed
at our sides, it was a blast, meeting it all cranium-first,
like academics, frothfoamgrit and the taste,
what was it, asphyxiation, psychedelic Escher
in blackwhite cubes, tableau enormous, picnic
tablecloth but undulating, spiked into color—crimson, canary—
until that last blow, ledge flat against
my mouth-hole, my whole body
condensed to one blinding exclamation point,
white protrusion of bone—white petals and light,
pearl-solid, luminous, all fourth-of-July and scattered,
pipe bombs bottle rockets Christmas crackers, oh,
what a party, annihilation, till the blue blue blue
palm sweeping my forehead, the hair from my forehead
and the ache of return, to the tenderness
of paint sable-brushed against silk, powdered
throat of the foxglove, flushed curve spiraling
into a conch, velvet crowning the doe's nose,
arms embracing the cello's hips, shoulders,
and what shudders from them, coaxed
or forced, distracted out of, with that bloodwhite flap
blinking at me from your cheek
and something in the eyes, maybe trout or bass or salmon
thrashing upstream, yellowglimmer and sickened,
we're not going to make it, we'll make it, *we're stranded,*
washed up on this hurricane shore, held together
by blood sticks and mud, oh paper, oh desks, oh treatises,

we weren't immune, on those banks, sky flat as anything,
a willowlike spider tree bending over us,
I focused on its branches, on the branches
of the branches, how comical that word *twig,*
surrounded by thousands of jokes as blood darkened
the silt like a cave painting

Voltage

Thunderhead's inhaled the oxygen
and I'm dodging raindrops to breathe.
Live wire held by yellow plastic clips
pens me in; it's the cows are free
under their corsets of flies,
breaking and entering
chlorophyll. Clovered
volts, stun and crackle of roots
and cells. The silo's flimsy
tin resounds when mourning doves
take wing. I've sent up a kite
with my tongue for the tail.
I'll make that current sing.

Galileo

One flight down they're fighting again,
really going at it, with much slamming
of doors and hurling of heavy objects,
and I've turned up my Bach but can still hear it
you're an idiot   don't talk about my stuttering,
I told you never to   fuck you just fuck you you fucking fuck
and it almost makes my own fights seem
civilized, as if I've finally learned something,
though it's more likely I simply lack the balls
I had 20 years ago, the righteous conviction,
my frontal lobe still a work-in-progress—
yes, that's the latest young-adult-research
breakthrough. I just read, too, that the venerable
right-left brain distinction is a fallacy,
maybe southpaws aren't really more creative
(a blow to my ego, but I will weather it—
especially as there are no longer stages of grief).
The wisdom keeps changing, jostling
the prior wisdom out of the nest
with entitlement and later amused and sometimes
tolerant condescension, the world was flat
and the sun went around, etc., etc.,
the burning chariots and the spirits
in the trees, the humours and the vapours
and the leeches, the lead-white
faces, the terror of the night
and terror of the day, which is why
we peopled them with gods, and music,

and science, and
get away from me you little bitch
you don't even have a job
and what is it about the word
Galileo that has such richness? It's parchment
and vinegar, ground glass and oiled copper,
it's the sun through a leaf jaundiced by autumn—
Isn't that what we do, stuff the void
with string theory or bling theory,
though we don't even know
where we put the keys last night,
or why no beauty's loud enough
to drown out rage and drown out sorrow.

The Prodigies

Lack of red meat made our blood run pale,
repelling mosquitoes and spider fangs
in this monument we called our home.

These were our lives: spread thin
and watery against a teeming push
of bodies: tangled braids, piglike
countenances, dimpled flesh
encased in sweaty cotton pleats.

They brought us vegetable pies.
They brought us boysenberries,
caviar, overripe cheeses on spotted silver
chargers lined with crisp doilies.

We could have been captured in overdetermined gilt
frames. We could have been hewn from Italian marble.
We could have been set down on scrolls
of finest parchment, scraped out with quills
plucked from plush white geese. Snowy cravats
tightened around our throats.

We had buttoners, escorters, morsel-tasters, skin-spongers.
Manicurists, soup-spooners, handkerchief-bearers.
Powderers, temple-pressers, cushion-testers.

Our heads were clear as consommé. Complexions
fair as paraffin. When we spoke—if we spoke—

our syllables fell like quicksilver beads
onto ice. They were sold in the markets
for thousands. They were peddled in faraway
villages, hoarded by housewives, traded
among children like cat's-eyes.

Kingdoms, empires. Mathematics bent its theorems
to the flecks in our eyes, and philosophy—
well, it took its subtleties from our bellies'
indelicate functions.

Each year I looked into the glass and saw my brother's face,
changing. Each year I recalled the pure white mouse
he'd found so long ago and tried to hide away
for fellowship, its sad pink clawing for air.

Eight questions

QUINCE

Squat and piggy, like the rest of him.
Barrel-body. Holding a hare by the ears
he tugs the skin off the meat,
relishing the *shhhh* of the fascia.
What's under the fur is a secret.
What's under the skin is divine.
Especially when brewed with port wine
and apple. Especially when roasted
with chestnut and quince. Do you ever
see yourself in the plush drain
of blood, in the marbled veins?
The figs are sweetest that have fallen
from the tree. The wasps with their jaws
bore holes in the slack meat.

TIMEPIECE

The cool intelligence of branches
casting shadows on a forest floor.
Cog by cog, dismantling the time
to make it run, balancing the jeweler's
file to hone a weightless wheel's
fine teeth. Spotless white, the lab,
impeccable as a tulip's petal.
How do you breathe, knowing

that even breath will tremble
the branches? *Nothing is more delicate*
than this whir of tungsten
and copper. It nestles in my palm
like feather and bone. Its heartbeat
the only one I hone.

GOSPEL

His hands were thick, meaty,
callused, but so gentle,
as one might imagine Picasso's.
They were tearing out
the pages of a hymnal.
When he was done
he floated them, one by one,
over the balcony. In the village
below, heaven glided down
on wide white wings.
What do you believe in?
Blowing a globe
from a monocle of soap,
igniting the soul of a cinder.

CANDLES

Impossibly long and tapered—
white candles in a chandelier.
With them she tore the bread
to pieces, scattering crumbs
the ants would soon hurry toward.
The palace doors were open
to a breeze of spearmint and lemon.
When the soldiers marched
through the olive groves,
did they know they marched
toward cages? *If you pierce*
the breasts of thrushes,
string them together on red twine,
they still sing the sweetest tune.

OIL

Shell-sloped, pearl-smooth, combing
her youngest daughter's hair
without a comb, separating strands
that snag, arranging them along her back
in a dark fan. The courtyard is surrounded
by coconut and banana palms, fat
glossy leaves giving shade the way
goats give milk. Did your mother

kneel behind you this way
to smooth the ripe slick oil
in your hair? *I closed my eyes*
and breathed in the certainty
of love moving through
my own black hair.

SPARKS, LIGHTS, AND DARKNESS

Two starfish brace against
the bathysphere's slopes
as it descends on its lifeline
of cable, swinging in currents
like a pendulum. *The red and the orange*
are as if they had never been,
and soon the yellow is swallowed up
in the green. And then the green
is gone. Two eyes spy through
fused quartz into the phosphorescent
gloom. What do you imagine
the universe to be? *Blue-blackness*
and sparks, then forever black,
the black pit-mouth of hell itself.

ARROYO

Cracked and leathery, curled
around reins worn smooth
with use, pulling left, then right.
And the familiar body beneath
obeys the silent intention.
In the bowl of the canyon
they pick their way through, surveying
dried creekbeds, deep fissures,
the blasted heartscape. After
cavalry devoured the land,
what sprouted in those miles
of conquering hoofprints?
When raindrops pelt the dust,
it's like a volley of gunfire.

COMPLEXION

Faultlessly filed ovals, half-
moons rising without a hint
of cuticle, buffed to baby's-bottom
gleam: his fingertips lightly
grip the brush's tortoise stem,
fanning *Rose Flirtation* or
Blushing Bride high on the white
cheekbone, rimming the lips

in *Peach Desire*. These portraits
that you paint on human skin—
Each time I bring a face to life
with perfect care I fall
in love, and die a little
every time it's buried.

After she told me she was pregnant

The body kept bobbing
to the surface so I slid her under
the ice, such a thin layer,
but it held, and she stayed there, fixed
in the flow of creekwater, rinsing
the blood from her, rinsing the lie,
which I only found out later,
once it was over, and then
I had a lifetime to think about it,
the few bubbles I saw collecting
under the ice, embedded
with bright yellow leaves.

So deeply that it is not heard at all, but

sister: the violin is blue. it plays stars, there was a field—

sister: that swelling in your belly will be a milkweed, a duty, a friend—

sister: goldenrod blossom: stippled ancillary: nonplussed bird—

sister: some of us need pain to shine.

sister: the cello bends with your love for it, that burden, it warps

the wood, the hollow in the wood, you've swelled the hollow in the wood:

sister: let go of those children and come with me, out to the edge

of this continent and stare out to sea:

sister: until a barge arrives to take you to the gleaming other edge

where lizards crawl and the brush is yellowgold and snakes whip up the dust—

sister: pick up this paper and pick up this pen—

sister: turn your face to me: i want to see more than half.

sister: roll up that grief, tie it off in silk ribbon, come out with me.

sister: take this hand and come into the prairie. sink down in the cattails.

sister: sit still enough, they'll forget you're there.

sister: i'll lend you my red-rimmed guitar.

sister: i was knocked off my feet by a black dog all briar and shag.

sister: you needn't lie in that sun-bleached collapse of linen.

sister: breathe through this straw, that's it.

sister: yes, you'll have those creases too. don't cry. don't cry.

sister: that's not the color i would have chosen.

sister: layers of parchment, they'll crumble at a touch.

sister: love all your images: they're smarter than you. they'll live longer,
they know how to.

sister: wrap yourself in barbed wire, blue leaves, and twine. in yellow paper,
white butter, in grasses.

sister: we enter the world this way. wide open: split: cracked open:

sister: feed yourself. the rest will be taken care of. promise

[ii.]

Daily, Weekly, Monthly

The tea canister is empty. I sustain myself
with whiffs of watered honey, in love
and the idea of love. Stealing another
newspaper is unnecessary; I already know
people live in bricks stood on end, end to end,
exhaling proof through charcoal throats.
Everything is rented.
                    Between walls
sway-backed under all that weight, a woman
slots herself into her vanity's chair and paints
her eyebrows on. In another room
a man pastes a handle on a bowl
and calls it a cup. Somebody affixes
tiny stars to her cracked blue ceiling, pleased
to find Orion.
                    Outside under a fast sky
a cement truck crests the hill. On the corner
two workmen compare the texture
of apricots. Potted pansies wilt
next to the watering can. My hand's
in the mailbox.

Pantoum

Little girl, your veins are showing through
your skin again. And again I will ignore it.
I will lay you down in the ordinary clover
and resume sex, our bored conspiracy.

Your skin again and again, I will ignore it—
although I can barely stand its blue-pink flush—
and resume. Sex, our bored conspiracy,
tethers me to the slim bent weed of your body

although I can barely stand. Its blue-pink flush
of fish's gills, albino snake's pellucid scales
tether me. To the slim bent weed of your body,
an artist might attribute the vulnerable beauty

of fish's gills, albino snakes' pellucid scales . . .
I am your husband. I can't see things the way
an artist might. Attributing "a vulnerable beauty"
is like a wry poem admiring its own cleverness.

I am your husband; I can't see things the way
I did before I knew you. Now my life
is like a wry poem: admiring its own cleverness,
it alienates the one who reads. I can't remember what

I did before I knew you, now. My life
a deconstructed text. What's the point of writing that

alienates the one who reads? I can't remember. What
can save us from seeing too much?

A deconstructed text—what? Is the point of writing that
our roles are judged irrelevant? Only love
can save us from seeing. Too much
rain has filled the mossy gutters; too many hours

our roles are judged: irrelevant. Only, love
returns me to this house at night, where
rain has filled the mossy gutters. Too many hours
spent feeling thunder rattle the iron bedframe

return me to this house at night, where
I'm like one treading water, mindless,
spent. Feeling thunder rattle the iron bedframe,
I mistake its tremble for my own—

I'm like one treading water, mindless
of the riptide, deadly current so strong
I mistake its tremble. For my own
long sweet strokes in the pale water

of the riptide—deadly current so strong—
pull me out to sea. And hold me
long, sweet. Stroke in the pale water
your mermaid's flesh: you belong here tangled in sea-reeds.

Pull me out to sea and hold me,
little girl. Your veins are showing through
your mermaid's flesh. You belong here. Tangled in sea-reeds,
I will lay you down in this extraordinary clover.

Song of the butcher's daughter

Can you imagine me, at middle age, still doing that?
Can you even imagine me at middle age.
White apron stained in cowsblood pigsblood chickenblood.
Oily gleam of the fat heap, studded with flies.

The smell always sickened me.
It doesn't come off, you know.
Steep in warm water and Ivory,
scrape under your nails with pins—
You'll always reek of innards.

Once I hit 13, in the raw blood
each month I felt like meat.
They looked at me like meat, leering over the glass
while I sawed through bone. I kept the knives sharp.
Better than sharp. Whetstone, grindstone. Dreamed
and dreamed.

The morning of my 16th birthday
I hopped the Greyhound to New York City
with all I could find in the till. I made my way,

met a rich guy. He says he'll put me through
veterinary school. His arm's around my shoulders
as we stalk the city and window
shop. There are the scarves that float
like rain about to fall. Enormous

sofas that'll survive apocalypse.
In one showcase are knives, well-oiled
and gleamy beside their leather sheaths.

Clean and clean and clean and clean and clean.

Apologia

Torrents of rain don't ask first, then assail
the ground, flooding burrows where shelter small
furred things. Spider, workmanlike, sets its snare
and waits for that cold pulse of insect heart.
Locusts don't dream of ruin as they descend
upon lush fields, no more than brushfire's spark
would contemplate the terrified stampede
of smoke-choked bodies, green cells charred to black.
The pack will leave behind a wolf so ill
he'd hinder on the hunt; a ribbonsnake
devours her own young should it stay near
instead of striking out. Sometimes a bee,
in self-defense—I wish I'd been kinder
to you—will die of its own baffled sting.

Blanket

He sold me off. *Claret,* he bellowed, *time to leave home now,*
I've found you a husband and he'll take you in. Claret, he hollered,
tuck up your things in this bag and run along the carriage is waiting.
Upstairs, now, folding, refolding worn cotton dresses, petticoats, the
picture book Mother gave me (pressed between pages 6 and 7,
a dried wildrose), a rag-lamb, embroidered pillowcase, Grandma's
claret glass thimble (*Hurry up!* barked from downstairs, nearly
buckling my knees), and only two bonnets would fit—oh—blue
calico with a ribbon of sky, peach with cherry grosgrain. I missed
the second step, caught myself hard with my heel on the third, but
down the rest thumped the overstuffed bag. A little wild in the eyes,
Father came running. Was it fear, there, under the raggedy brows?
Claret was all he said, apology, admonishment, and it had something
of Mother's tone in it, a frown and a groan. I wouldn't look at him
again. *Claret—*

       and now it *was* Mother's voice, taking
my hand, holding it close to the coals, *you must never,*
never—and it was steadying me as I tiptoed
to the edge of the lake, grub-white toes bulging
under the surface, it was lifting my tangled long hair and
dragging the pearl-handle brush through, it was feeling
my forehead sticky with fever, it was stinging
against my bottom, it was singing its own songs
in the bath, with the sponge and lard soap, it was turning
the pages of a picture book, it was poking a needle through
the hem I'd torn, it was shoving me from the back
on the long way to church, it was pinching

dough all round the edge of a pan, it was never
touching Father, not even to fix his collar, it was turning
over, and over, a yellow telegram, it was gripping
the edge of the watering trough, it was making the gesture
that meant *stop, not now, I don't want you, leave me be,*
it was twisting a dead head off a marigold, it was burning
against rope from the well, it was brushing crumbs
absent-mindedly into the other hand, it was finding
its way to her mouth, covering her mouth,
it was pointing, *get out, get out,* it was propping her up
against the back of a chair, it was holding the knee
she'd just fallen on, shattered, it was tapping my face
gentle as a spiderweb, it was dropping glasses
and silverware, it was tugging up the blanket
to her chin, over her eyes, over her forehead
till all I saw was the top of her skull, it was
opening and closing and opening like a fishmouth,
just like a fishmouth pulled off the hook
and then it was the claw tucked under the blanket
and taken away, and replaced by Father's thick hand,
heavy on my shoulder or my waist or my thigh,
fingers raking my hair with always that tremor to them,
while I stood stock-still as if it would stop.

Annunciation

Cherries hemorrhage in their bowl.
Dough bloats beneath its damp
tent of hours and a clump
of basil wilts on the windowsill,
scabbed in aphids. A marbled rib-eye
slab gleams stickily. Cat's licking
himself, one eye on the meat. Knives
lean easy in their butcher-block
slots. Husband's home, and greeted
smilingly. She hears the rush
of far-off waves and levers
to her knees, forehead bruising
bleached linoleum. An angel's burning
hands hold down her shoulders.
The cat goes for the meat.

Library

I dream a sonnet made of buttons. Star-
shaped; faceted jet; fabric bristled pink;
one boasts a lurid trompe l'oeil cardinal
posed stiff against its milky plastic sky.
Paired off, their colors rise and fall, like breath—
a verse no doubt penned by the selfsame clerk
who, disgruntled (refused promotion, perk,
or punch-card-less lunch hours), now arrogates,
upends, and reconstructs the library
by spine color. The emeralds here; rubies
just there; and the voluminous onyx
of all that flaccid pulp. Then, dazed with pride,
with anarchy's frank gorgeousness, sinks
down among the transformed stacks, and weeps.

Want Me

Lemons crystallized in sugar, glistening
on a blue-glazed plate. The rarest volume
bound in blood leather. A silk carpet
woven so finely you can't push a needle through,
that from one edge is the silver of a leaf
underwater, and from the other bleu lumière,
first frost on the cornflowers. A duet for cello
and woodsmoke, violin and icicle. Tangle of
black hair steeped in sandalwood, jasmine,
bergamot and vetiver and jewelled
with pomegranate seeds. Panther's broad tongue
soothing hunt-bruised paws. Eyelids of ribbonsnakes.
Taut skin of a lavender crème brûlée. Split
vanilla pods swollen with bourbon. A luna
moth's wings, enormous, celadon, trembling.

Noon shadow

Amazed at such new magnets
in the skin, in flecks of gold
caught in her hair (he wants to touch it),
in a fine scratch along the pig's belly
of her cheek, the tracing of blood
and a faint upwelling of flesh surrounding it
(he wants to run his tongue against it
for the salt, he is so suddenly terribly thirsty),
he turns to her and grips her upper arms, hard,
and backs her up against the barn wall,
wondering at the ease he's felt with her
all his life without knowing it,
and in the instant of his knowing it, that joy
utterly gone, utterly lost—and this new thing,
this her about to struggle (he can feel it),
is all he wants, maybe all he's wanted:
the moment when the hare
looks up from grazing, petrified,
then bounds headlong for cover in the brush.

[iii.]

Anaphylaxis

The wasp there again when I surfaced:
those dangling legs, the budlike head,

lethal black thorax drilling
inches from my lake-clogged ear.

I dove beneath and swam, again,
to the limits of my breath, through

the bath-warm surface, through
cold current. Out of our element,

what other story is there—pursued,
pursuer, panic in the long strokes?

The death that insect carried
was not the one I wanted. And oh,

I wanted death, or thought I did: days spent
twitching a razor at my wrists,

cuddling a little mortuary of pills
in my palm. Yet when it came

I swam from it as any prey.
There was still something left to want.

Dictator

The quail are back: the big quail,
and the smaller quail, scurrying
to keep up. They're pecking in the garden,
rooting for seeds or grubs or whatever
quail root for. They're absurd, these birds,
apostrophes bobbing from their heads,
burbling staccato in their collective fright.
Each time I see them, I feel lulled,
lazy, enormous. Each time it's like
watching puzzle pieces of myself
scattering for their lives,
and yet here I am, above it all,
leaning against the porch railing,
sipping a cool glass of lemonade, coolly
noting that for all the terror of their collective flight
it sounds like nothing so much as umbrellas opening.

Rough

Stars cluster, discarding light like garbage.
The stale air reeks of rain-soaked hay, the fields'
slow ruin. I rock myself on the porch swing,
poulticed by crickets' pulsing drone. Last week
it was against the fridge, long handle dug
along my back, another spine. He loves
an edge: railing, doorway. He's made me kneel
in the gravel. Last night it was my rump
near-punctured by the baby's-room doorknob
and I pushed back, but only roused him more.
Sometimes it's dark and muscular, the pain.
Sometimes it's sweet: can't tell his skin from mine.
Say what you like— even when he's gone
he holds me where he's bruised me like a plum.

Trouble.

Trouble on the prairie,
in the bending heads of the queen
anne's lace. Among the long, long grasses
flailing. And the monarchs' wings
above it all, their newly flustered
pulse. He comes along the path,
off the path, swiping the bobbing heads
from his way, the lavender cones,
dust-pink brooms, and the spiders
strung in them. Boots flatten the blades
and behind him green struggles
to close itself up. He crosses the marshes,
arms out in front to part cattails that dare
to rise taller, a flurry of displaced wings.
He'll find that doll he lifted to the swing
and pushed until her feet touched the sun.
He'll find the girl whose both hands
fit his one, whose very lace sang *pure*
in summer as in winter, whose eyes
were clear as marbles shot from his grubby
fingers, the fingers of boyhood
friends. Whose skin ripened till he could
barely see. He's reached the woods
now and the sentinels of trees are whispering
won't give her back and the floor is more shadow
than light, the very creek with its crayfish
gurgling *ours now* and then *his now*
and what sky there is reeling with new

certainty, and he kneels in the jewel-
weed its jestercap blooms, ridiculous
pods exploding with seeds, and the ferns
rise till they meet the leaves
and the dizzy leaves
spread to meet the vines
and he kneels and he kneels
in that green confusion.

Barn Door

What dream? What hope? What
white rope coiled into a smile
around the throat? What
white sheet? What yellow shadows?
What about the barn door
swung open in the heat? What about
the straw scattered on the floor,
the hook, the rusted hook?
What of complacent faces
of the cows, sweet smell of hay,
the milk? What of the handle
of the rake? The plow?

Built It Ourselves, Out of Love
and a Few Nails

Solid things like butter and leaves,
dough and forgiving, I want to rise
and smell bread and be next to you
in our house in the middle of a field

You'll milk the cows with cold morning hands
and a ribbon checked blue and white
or red and white is in the wind,
not attached to anything,
just fluttering in its own way

The eggs are still warm
you put your hands over my eyes
and I know what it is you want me for
Eggs and bacon, always bacon,
your heart is fat

Beans, snap beans, peas clustered,
growing together, sweet
with their little bellybuttons
peas in halves, shellinghalving peas,
oh god, peas

There is anxiety, and wheat blowing
I want to insert a grasshopper, sun in the fabric—
the ladybugs looking up at us with a love so great
we don't know how the world
doesn't just burst on its axis—

I'll comb my hair by the river,
comb the petals from my hair,
smoothing the surface with those white petals
till the fish swim up, all wings and tails
to watch their sky go white

There was an angel
we built together
newborn skin, a sac of light
there was a joke about an angel
it was the most delicate thing we had

When we met
there were grasses, the smell
of motor oil, hum of the motor,
my hands on your thighs, your hips,
and the very air held us up

You love the way I smell,
you lick my hands, I rub my smell
into your eyes, your cheeks,
your mouth is more,
there's too much to it

Too much to remember, I writhed for 2 hours
on the old sheets

The Night Orchard

I. LOSING GRAVITY

Someone is saying *the body*
is an irredeemable thing. Don't tell me how
to pray: I'm stripped like wallpaper, weak
gum and sweet glue. I've seen whole
houses arranged by the colors of their roofs.
Behind these lids a stippled orchard
revolves in the sun's decrease. Fruit
refuses to fall. Swelled walnuts split
like words, hulls still propped in branches of
their beginning. Steady myself with handfuls
of air. Over that wall I know it's winter,
someone saying *the taste of your tongue*
in your mouth is the only poem.

II. THE NIGHT ORCHARD

Wound through Winters, past
the old graffitied Stevenson bridge,
in the headlights, ghost imprint, orchard
retina repeating: angel-bright trunk
and the black sweeping tail . . .
film-frame symmetries. Then a crook
in the road struck like a snake
I never saw.

        (What I mean to say is this:)
White stitches pulled the lanes together.
The road curved, but I was all angles.

Reflectors' glare—a startled deer's
mirrored eyes?—and the sweet, thin air
of panic. The dark blurred itself in:
leaden thighs, feet dead among
the pedals. All those tiny sequins
of glass.

       And then the bodying
trees bent over me, soldierly, kindly,
bidding me to count one branch
for each heartbeat (*I am, a splinter,
I am, a point of light*) until the red
sirens came.

III. AN ORCHARD

                     is not a body. Not
the sticky accumulation of claw,
vein, sight-globe, hole, and bone.
An orchard is not a bellowed, symmetrical,
hinged flapping science of limbs, nor
the tethered suck/expel of cells—
not an unbalanced head on a stalk, or
toes digging in individual cockpits
for balance.

       A body's not these rows
of humbled, knurly dwarfs economizing
sunlight, rationing it to a basketweave

on the stunted grass. Bodies aren't
planted at intervals; near, but not
touching, trimmed when leaves threaten
to scrape their aluminum palms. We don't
walk through the body calculating loss,
or profit, according to the weight
of its boughs—

IV. HARVEST

Crates stacked against the sun,
stenciled, singular. Heart and belly
of the wood serve the fruit
of its body, of a brother's—

I think pain is like that.
Nerve upon nerve, stapled
and bolted. Stacked against
the season. An arithmetic.

V. ROWS

Irrigated, sprinkled, tilled,
mulched, staked, trimmed,
hovered-over. Entered.
In the orchard all paths
are clear and straight.

Mow comb pluck
claw prune spray
until the boughs are heavy
with effort, until we bend,
we fall, we crack open—

VI. DEATH IN AN ORCHARD

How would it? Succumb.
Can a body stop from too much
symmetry? Nouned under saw, under axe,
reduced by wasps, by canker veins—

(And if now, against crisp hospital linen,
a plastic clip ticks my pulse to peaked red lines?
In the mattress these elbows leave dents
like little funnels. Pink soldered body:
tugging at the hems of my gown, I cover
the scars like long and formal
opinions.)

I am a splinter, I am
a point— Too far, or not far
enough: trunk sealed, or flayed open
to hunger in the loosening light. Can I live
with that? And what else—

VII. TELLING

In this incomprehensible, alphabet light
I'll step down from silence: what's in my mouth is that
I still want to lay you down in that slatted orchard
light, to tuck us there, thin husks between air-breathing
roots and earth-bound branches. What sweeter than
watered hay steaming off the fields? Crows stutter
by the road's haunches. Tractors chug, slow till
of chaff-dulled blades. Over the wall we find
it's summer, we live on less.

[iv.]

White Mushrooms

The sun uses the leaves
like a strainer. What gets through
is language. It tastes of cool earth and sand,
smells a little of truffles. Resting
under the trees— not resting,
the light moves as the leaves
move— let's stop there. I can't say
what language is, where it goes,
the connection between the fists
of the fir tree and the platters
of the slim oak that reveal
the achingly gentle lift and fall
of the wind. I've never understood
the wind, its invisible force
in this world. Like gravity.
I can stare into the woods for days
pulling into that green blur
my own nonsense—feel
the trees on the outside of the stand
swaying while those inside are protected,
wishing to see only green but knowing
below, the slices and chips of brown,
deadnesses, and above, a kind of blue,
cloudy, clear, you name it—
gray-blue, marine-blue, sky-blue
sky, oh the painters are creative—
I used to think naming was knowing.

The ferns explode, they're not fiddle-
heads but something else that grows
not by uncurling but by expansion—
that's not it either. They start out
small and grow in direct proportion
till they're bigger. I want to say now
lust is like that too—maybe, but lust defies
proportion, bulging innumerable
ways, like an animal trying to force
out of a balloon's walls. Mushrooms
prod their ways from the slackened soil
after it rains, little white noses. Now I've fallen
out of it. Or it just can't get through.

Wind sonnet

Tsumuji chinook baguio monsoon;
waimea zephyr wiffet gust buran.
Levanto leveche zonda simoom,
sirocco (cat's-paw flurry) huracan.

Makani batash vento coado—
matsukaze nor'wester bull's-eye squall.
Upepo hio bise solano,
kurma serak baridi williwaw.

Kazkazi bobeni fuvallat shum
oprollen yel. Willy-willy datoo
osuruk venterello szel frist vind,
ruwach tuuli ani mistral haboob.

Meltemi blases aquilo typhoon—
flaw equinoctial I tien tien fung.

Ghazal

His hands moved to her thighs. One word: "Permission?"
She closed her eyes; she opened her permission.

To make the tea called *Yin Hao* or Silver Tip,
five times the jasmine's asked for its permission.

Pulled over her like patchwork, different bodies,
different beds. Frailty, thy name is permission.

Food's savor lies in spice, in fire, in friction;
forget the salt. The pepper's your permission.

2 flat 2 thin 2 lure boys in 2 loving,
she waited for her body's own permission.

Spraypaint's just the need to see your name scrawled large—
If only those damned cops would give permission.

Ruidos matrimonios, noche buena:
She sinks down in cushions of white permission.

A horse paws at the red ground. As his back hooves
clear barbed wire, he's not thinking of *permission*.

Eurydice chomps on a ripe persimmon.
She's wallowing in love's denied permission.

Mama never used to let us out the house.
Now Mama's dead. All we got left's permission.

"Does the wind say, 'I'm too tired'? Do the waves
say, 'I'm too tired'? Love, dear, is permission."

What is death but the home-safe of body's dream?
The body gives the soil its permission.

Pardon the bee who drowns in her own honey:
you, flower, gave this Honeybee permission.

Aquarium

These girls wear sex like lipstick. I think
this one's the Undead. Heavy-lidded,
pawing the air like a drugged kitten,
stilettos piercing holes in the scuffed-up
linoleum. I'll bet she tastes like
a red paper valentine. No, lemon
on a cut tongue. I try to lose myself
in the muffled beats through the glass.
A succulent chicken-thigh shimmies past,
dimpled softly like a golf ball. That vampire won't
look at me. Wall-eyed, carp-eyed. I've been here too long
soaking in the slot-machine atmosphere. I think of
what's not waiting for me at home. What if
Elvira here's really a sweet homemaker,
come to bring me my slippers and paper
and walk the dog twice a day rain or shine?
No, she's coming at me like a bat, dissolving
the glass like gelatin, knocking me to my knees.
Poor blue Chuck's never gonna be seen again
at the office noosed in his trout-silly tie,
experimenting with paper cuts and binder-clip
nipple clamps. Has anything changed
since I was a kid? My lunchmeat urges,
my baffled jeans. My pimp breath, my laboratory
kisses. Nope. Not much. In the aquarium a butter clam
floats by, soothing, the way it takes its time,
going nowhere, and the girl it's attached to,

soothing too, a manageable storm of boredom
and sex, now headless, now armless, pressing
against the glass, white anonymous lullaby half-
babydoll, tottering on skyscraper heels, oh
I want something so beautiful I forget my life.

Sky-Blue, Grass-Green

Wait. It will come to you—
the unexpected *frisson,*
the trees chock-full
of tailfeathers and eyes.
If you stand stock-still
in the pencil-shadow
of a birch— O I am
amazed by the wind,
allowed to stroke anything
anywhere it wants.
If a wind lifts your
skirt, to whom will you
complain? Compassion,
the wise man said, is
holy. I felt a great
expansion in the heart
region whenever a certain
R. appeared; it was
a kind of internal
breeze pulling outward—
later I refused to call it
"love." The day starry
with milkweed, a peeling
red barn shoved up
against the sky's rude
blue, and equally in
the neon, unreal grass—
Why doesn't anyone churn

butter anymore? What
is homemade now?
Not even the news. My dog
knows this and buries the paper
before we get to it. Daily
we thank him.

Love & Distance

Sleigh-burns in snow: you're in New York,
behind chrome counters hawking pork-filled buns
to strangers. I'm in an orange grove, hands
sticky with oil from the rinds and dark
from smudging. I'm wedded to the ripe sun
that hangs these branches heavy; you're ravished
by that grey stain of a town. We're tragic:
whipsmart Ma Bell gets fat off our longing
while our bank accounts waste too lean to spawn
a ticket. Suits me fine. What do I miss?
On New Year's Eve we meet in Morocco
and make love in unprecedented ways,
our lips pressed tight to plastic. You're grubby,
I'm sour, and this whole grand world's at peace.

New Dominion

The pond breathes out the seclusion of another afternoon
unvisited by bodies. Everything is quiet but ugly—
not in the sense of its banks heaped
in decaying muck or sodden sportsocks,
but more like the leathered faces of the farmers
in those FSA photos from the Depression.
They didn't look resigned, exactly—just didn't know
there were alternatives, so realness shined out of them.
It's always seemed odd to me that at the vanishing point
of ugliness lies its opposite, that euphoria's tenor
is that of despair. Maybe we are limited in our truths,
and Ecclesiastes had it right. Maybe the sun
ringing this pond and its black collar of trees
is the one bad habit I don't have to unlearn. Now
the *kop-plunk* of some silly fish calls attention to itself
and it's the suspicious hard look of an eye toward the camera,
hard but carrying light, while the better-off are roving about
with their flashing gadgets and fancy suits, puffing
and sweaty and coffined in corn-dust. I promise myself
not to translate this pond, to let it be, downtrodden
and junk-filled but at least what it's always been.
Scummy surface traversed by waterbugs,
the clots of mosquitoes, tangly jungle of weeds
and rotting vines. It has no aspirations. It's a relief.

Allergy

The ragweed, the goldenrod, the lady's slipper, the queen anne's lace, the figwort. Bald lousewort, scaly finnegan, popcorn mouse pea, scarlet monkey flower, duck potato. Demon-blossom, horse-brute, dog-mange, lemon-pepper, careful-sward, peach-juice-drip, orange-tipped runnynose, longbottomed boatflower, lover's lips, elvis's hips, vampire mousepod, boston joy. Leaping jester's hose, unhinge-me-not, missed-a-step, careful-now, pearly nevermore, wild mead, sock's breath, harlequin grass, wheelbarrow heart, hangman's-noose, sparrowthroat, talk-too-much, gypsy's fringe, cabbagesquat, cloud cheek, rampant bitterweed, pup's-mint, glass-o-milk, jar-o-paint, can-o-beans, old-man's bunion, buttered rumpkin, buxom ladypainter, coiled snakewort, spinster's pod, pinch-faced hollowseed, boiling-oil gloss, shivering rembrandt's nose, leaping cellophane, something's-crawling-on-you, half-mast tasselberry, dead man's claim, the blackeyed don't-press-charges, the soupy-eyed mary, the coy-faced petticoat-drop, the empty-lantern-flower, bat-winged underbelly, four-glossed harrowtongue.

Dead heat

through which a cry rises — fealty — pressed
& raw & ululated rose serrated leaf
stalk & Japanese maple rotted into
the sidewalk, so many reds you lifted
like a truck's mudflap the silhouette girl leaning back
taunting her chest at you that ass round
& plump — grab it before it's leaves
heaped in the gutter, grab it before it's straw &
cinders — the rocking chair took me somewhere
else, i coveted the arcs of birds' wings — the backs
between the wings — i wanted to rest
my cheek there, as they flew, pumping
those bones into flight,
feathers bones motion, disturbing the light
into pulse, bruising land & the fields
smudging grasses & powdered wings & buzzing &
sighs in an afternoon gone crisp & burny —
chaff chaff chaff, we've invented
ourselves into a diffusion —
of tenderness — how i was held — with both
hands at my hips — & pulled in —
because that's what there was — in the
intimacy, like a thin skim of glass —
i mean ice, that season — lacing leaves,
lake's heartbeat beneath, current
pulsing the ice, burning breathe-holes —
oh the toe wants to test it, step through,
hear it shatter & crack — bone-crack

as the blood seeps up —
wild red berry translucent as glass in a beak
curved goldenrod — ringing light & soon —
soon after — don't bargain, just give it
to me, i'm falling, unfamiliar, paint
clumped on the canvas, my hands in it,
wanting — these hands, slide them
through — anything — wishes — glass jars —
a window — convex wings — crisp —
give it to me, the answer
under my house, a story — nanny goat
flush from the fields, udder powdered in
frost — grass, brittle — borrow borrow —
grape-purple — fruit crushed in the —
seeder, de-seeder, paint, orange,
a canvas, & your hands on it — its
white surface, marking me —
oh, i want it — your hands all
ink & blond haste — it's like spelling, i want
so to do it right, our names
this way, & blank canvas —
story in weave & gesso — flakes off,
the white plaster, a bend in a leaf
wanting water, it rippled, the page, as
my eyes closed, the story, forget it —
they're closing — grey, pel, pelican,
nosebleed, illegible, ask me — i never could
shrug it off, this body, no, knowledge

of this body, i watched
myself over & over letting you feel me,
letting you feel, watched watched watching
from somewhere (i wasn't —
there — on the ceiling, perhaps,
behind your eyes —
milky & blue-rimmed &
clear, & forgiven —
valse a mille temps — madeleine —

finally had an emotion
but i dropped it
into a story
that wasn't mine —

a glass of water

with a hole in it

Vultures at Cold Canyon

And now that steady
shhhhh, a knife-edged whistle
announcing what vision can't
conceive: they are descending
in a shape that is exactly your own
fear, the actual feathers' flip and mess
and the body's plummet through
what-is-no-longer-air, but also
body, and the sheer resist of weight—
that sound, and the talons,
and the red throat, the hooked beak
that rips a slit in the sky
and enters it.

Rough honey

Bee-stung, kerosene sister, kneeling
saint: in the smackdown, the allegory,
the happy ending: she wore lipstick,
she wore red heels, she wore tunes
from the jukebox. Behind the gas station,
in the gravel, between boats moored
to their pickups, with her palms out, collecting
rain. It wasn't rain, her knees
were bruised, sweet reek
of gasoline, of dust and clover.
Gold ring, milk carton, cigarette.
Black root and cinder.
What did you ask for,
oh honeyfied, tangerine
sister? I used to watch you
with the lipstick, the gestures
in the mirror. The way your legs crossed,
the skirt creased, the sun and thunder.
Where did you go? I remember you
walked like a soldier.

Ground Fire

We sat together under the only tree, laced
into the field to catch lightning, there wasn't any
lightning, only that tremor running between your hand
and my thigh, I didn't move, pretended it wasn't
happening, a leaf fell and caught
in your collar, I loved that, I stared at it,
feeling the small flame on my thigh, it barely moved
but spread, the weight—barely weight—of your fingers
together on the skin, just under the edge of my skirt,
grasses tickling underneath, edge of that leaf
catching the sun, losing it, catching it again—
I was tired, a little, in the sun, wanted to lean back
and let the tree hold me up, all those roots or years—

II.

Green land, green thoughts, take this from me:
the fire's burning too high and I'm afraid, tinder,
twine, what binds us together is so close, I'm frightened
of stones heating, the veins of fire beneath the soil
that hide, leap out, engulf the field, the sleeping dogs,
my grandmother's house, we couldn't save it
and the beams collapsed, tremor, the neighbors
felt it half a mile away, heard it and ran, dragging buckets,

but what could douse a conflagration like that?
It was beautiful, god, a field set afire
by the sun, and smoke so thick
it blotted out the moon—

Halo

A swirl of it: a stain, like cinnamon:
that's how it was, at the base
of her skull, radiating like a halo.
I watched, for a long time, her outline,
her shadow, her second self
sink into sand. They say the soul
lifts from the body; that it takes wing
from sullied matter, a perfumed storm,
petals and light. I saw a slackening,
a gradual collapse to paleness tinged
in yellow, in slate. A lowering, not a lifting
as the earth that once held her up
loosened to take her in. A sigh.
Then a quiet that was more than quiet,
a listening that itself became like noise.

Our Campaign for Her World

I'm aching my way up the back road, the long steep
low-gear bit that kills me every time,

when a red car goes by, slow, the driver
turning his head then moving on.

I'm not much nearer the top
when he comes by again and stops

and mumbles something ... *college* ...
Sweet Briar? "Yep, right across the highway,"

I reply, though who could be on this excuse
for a road and not know where the college is—

in a town that *is* the college—
is beyond me. He drives off and his words

go up and down with the pedals until it's clear
he'd asked me if I went to college there. Maybe

he's some wealthy daddy champing at the bit
to scold the campus cops for letting well-bred girls

so far off rein? Maybe. I coast past spindly brambles
bent beneath wild blackberries' promise,

ditches spiked with thistle, padded in pink clover
blossom. On both sides, towering crazy and triumphant,

kudzu topiary bathes in golden light. I stop to watch
a stopped train chug beneath the wooden bridge

—each time I cross this bridge I wish for trains—
and in the heat, the cadence of the interrupted

train, I hear a gravel-scrape beside me
and it's his red Chevrolet. I get a good eyeful:

moustached and balding, maybe 50, so fat he's melting
into the seat of his red Chevrolet.

After a long moment he drawls
you wanna make you some money?

You wanna make you some money: what
lurid porn frames flicking through this guy's skull

compelled him to circle round twice in his big ol' car
to see if he couldn't score his own Lolita?

*Fade in. A sweet young thing hunched over in the front seat
sucks my sweaty cock*

This isn't the Strip, it's lush, rural Virginia,
just round the bend from an arts center—

not to mention that well-endowed girls' school
whose students bring to campus their own horses,

trotting to the motto "Our Campaign for Her World"—
and I almost ache for him,

for how we can dream ourselves
so deep we're just plain lost. One part of me

wants to ask *how much,* to lean down close
and breathe *d'ya want me to suck your sweaty ol' cock,*

mister? oh yeah, I bet you do. Because
I'm not above cruelty, I'm not above

a story. Yet a man like this may have a shotgun
on his front seat, a man like this may have

rope coiled by his boots, so what comes out is *no*
with such frank disgust you'd think even a man like this

would flush with shame, would limp home to his just-fine wife
and daughter—what do you bet he has a daughter?—

and buy them things and treat them nice and nurse
his tail between his legs. But his expression doesn't change

and he coasts down the long hill I've just struggled up,
maybe humming to himself, maybe feeling like a hero.

Robber girl

I took what I needed and nothing more—
not that last gold bracelet, fine as a braid
twined from three strands of a child's hair,
not that ruby tear, clear and faceted
as a pomegranate seed—just a blouse with gold
threads, just a coat with red glass buttons.
They always said I was too smart
for my own good and good only for
making trouble. And I thought *trouble?* What
a beautiful word, half of *troubadour*—
wineskins, ballads, riotous by the canals
with much lifting of skirts and telling
of tales—syllables strung like pearls
on a backbone of half-light and gain.

Blue Tiles

Cat's eyes a hard amber and I'm thinking
of you. Plants outgrow me eating air.
The windows won't shut. Steam hisses
empty. I want more doors. More light.
An image drowns in a pool somewhere
in Morocco, gold flash of a fish's scale,
tiles blue underwater. Blue shade and then
the sun choking on petal after petal. Your nose
deep in it. This citrus breeze and again. Bitter
rind sucked off your fingers, dip them through
the surface and watch how long ripples need
to reach the other side. Lean heavy
against flesh firm as an olive's slick with its own
oil. Chew the leaves I bunch in my fists,
coil their stems round my fingers. Stay.

Clearing the Field

The yellow pail sits
on a white stoop. The wallpaint
is peeling a little, vertically,
the curls catch shadows, bluish,
like a shadow on milk, a little cat
laps at it, no wait, it's just a shadow
on the wall, and the cat is across the field,
bounding after a dun-grey mouse
with a long tail, a tail easy enough to pounce on,
but the mouse wedges itself between the blades
of the plow and the cat goes mad
with frustration, thrusting one paw
then the other between those rusted
blades, batting at the mouse,
which has pressed itself
nearly flat against the ground
and if you were close you'd see it
trembling, really shaking, nosetip
to tail, as the cat does what cats do,
then hears a hollow bell's *clankclank*
and bounds away home, leaving the mouse
to a few more days of mouseness,
and leaps onto the porch and waits
for its meal, which it always gets
soon after the ringing of the bell.
It's like that day after day, scraps
on a plate, white edged in green
ivy, a ring of ivy green and blue,

the sun catches a particular corner
of the porch and lights up the cracks
between the boards, splinters,
what's fallen between, under the house
there are centuries of living, millipedes
and such, wide awake in the dark,
and below, more life stuffed into the soil
that supports those who live in the house,
which they built from the ground, or their
grandparents; there are cows stamped onto
the glasses on the breakfastable, the legs
are unsteady and the glasses rattle a bit,
the plates, the eggs slide, their suns
getting runny, in the middle of the table
is a bunch of hydrangeas, bruise-purple
and tired, we rake our hands through them,
through these days, quiet with sun
and cracks in the earth and wheat
the color of our hair and burnt cheeks
and a solitude we take for granted, here
against the paint-blue sky speckled
with a tree or two on this, our land,
our gift, our four corners, what we work
and long for and reinvent,
year after year— I feel a little sorry
for the cat, who can't get everything
he wants, everything he runs after,
for the mouse, who lives a life of hiding,

for the long blades of grass that fall beneath
the plow. I clear the field, pull together
some love and forgetting and mulch it
into the rich soil, a miracle it gives back,
sun or rain it finds a way, I've never
understood that, the constancy—oh I know
that's not true but I want it—to depend
on an earth giving forth torrents of wheat
and masses of flowers and taut gleaming
crops, an earth steady under your feet,
always, from the day you hide
beneath your mother's apron to the day
you tie those strings around your waist
to the day they flutter on the clothesline
with no one to wear them.

Holding

Those close to me go gray. But I'm
watching the fog cotton the hills,
swallow seagulls; the wind's pale
do-si-do with the treetops of the eucalyptus.
Little things. The cilantro seedling
choked by its own soil, windowsill's
persisting trail of ants, the clinging
ivy's suctioned feet. Grizzled
wing of a crow that lands on the *C*
of the balcony. It takes so much
to pull together this fabric, maintain
its spidered traplines. Who has time
to notice shadowed gestures, new terrain
etched in the mirror? What we love is near
enough. We focus on the hills.

Ars poetica

Bereft! Because of this or that.
Caught strangely, hooked in the chest.
Anatomized, wept. Kept keening

in this room or that. Adrift,
as if left lonely on some leaky
skiff and bound to wrack or ruin.

Fore, aft: mantas, jellys, sharks,
not sustenance, nor company. Just this:
what if to be left were gift? The luck

to shuck the shell, emerge
virginal. Without what's gone,
what's birth? Explorers

make their reports in foam
or frost then perish, leaving behind
fresh colonies. Here's mine.

(How to Fall from) Grace

It's as easy as whistling
to a man in a pickup truck, letting him
put his hands on your hips,
letting him touch your face
with his whiskery lips

it's as easy as listening to the nonsense
of somebody oh,
so much younger than you
as he traces the map of spider veins
behind your knees, and up your thighs
entranced by the way the blood ends there

easy as whispering
to the pear trees *i once fell here,*
ripe as a felled pear,
sticky with wasps—
i once lay here
with a boy
on top of me
in the sun
in the slatted light
that comes between the leaves
in the latest afternoon—

it's as easy as forgetting
where you put the keys
and it occurs to you it's just the last

in a string of things
your mind has let go
dropping like marbles
in the spaces between your fingers
one by one to roll away in clear glass
infinity

as easy as turning over a shell,
flipping it over to see what's underneath
and pocketing it, and walking away
across the aching sand

it's as easy as—once you get a grip
on the tip of one feather
of one wing—pulling him down,
putting your hands on those shoulderblades and
keeping him down, it's as easy as stroking
the feathers of the angel
till he does what you want, till he wants
exactly what you want

as easy as taking
the hand of a boy
and walking through the orchard, stepping over
each shadow of each trunk, the basketweave,
keeping the luck that you have
as the hair sweeps across your shoulders
& your back

and he puts his hand in your hair and
pulls you to him by the back of the head
and you sway in the orchard light
and you kiss in that orchard light
and the air is still and silent
except for a pair
of redwinged blackbirds
off in a tree at the edge of the stand

easy as the way your thighs
stick to the seat on a searing summer day
the way your skin seals to the vinyl
and the noise it makes
when you peel yourself off it
and slide your hands down
to pull off the sweat
that's gathered there

it's as simple as taking the curve too fast
so the tires squeal,
hands gripping the wheel so tight, almost
almost going too fast
and just violating the center line
just transgressing the center line

simple as buying the most expensive meat
the largest, leanest cut of filet mignon
pointing and saying *that one, please*

at $26.99 a pound, *that one's for me,*
i deserve that

simple as throwing out a pen
that isn't finished yet,
that's been used to wish things
away that you didn't ask for,
that's been used to ask for
what you've never had
that's been used to build words
out of strangers, out of the backs
of cars, out of bracelets dangling silver
and light on the most delicate wrist
held very softly
by a rougher hand
warmed by the sun
scratched by dried grasses and straw

it's as easy as wanting too much
as the sun sears the grasses
to straw, bleaches them gold
and aware, gold and awake,
bleaches them to brushfire, waiting
to happen, in the core,
in the seeds, in the hollow
in the center of the straw

as easy as wrapping your legs around
a boy you now love
and pushing harder, saying *for me, for me*

easy as dropping what you've worked on
all these years as if it were a marble falling
from your hand, as if it were a straw,
poised at the end of a lit match
as if it were a bird with one wing
clipped, lurching in the air-earth air-earth

as cleaving to a remembered night
in the stiff summered air
hands sliding past your waistband,
warm and urgent, drawing closer
in a quiet
punctuated only by katydids
announcing themselves
in the blackness

and letting him
for there's no moon tonight
to show what goes on between the rows,
the spiders strung across
and holy
in their appointed tasks—
ours, too, to thrash

wholly in the chaff
overwhelmed
with the beginnings
of gratefulness,
trusting
with a whole life

most of which
is still ahead

Acknowledgments

Grateful acknowledgment is made to the editors of the publications in which the following poems first appeared, some in slightly different form:

32 Poems: "Dictator," "Want Me"

Alaska Quarterly Review: "Sky-Blue, Grass-Green"

The American Poetry Review: "Daily, Weekly, Monthly," "Losing gravity"

Best New Poets 2009: "Eight questions"

Calyx; Many Mountains Moving: "Holding"

Cimarron Review: "Aquarium"

Green Mountains Review: "Anaphylaxis," "Apologia," "Ars poetica," "Galileo," "Noon shadow," "So deeply that it is not heard at all, but," "Voltage"

The Greensboro Review: "Love & Distance"

Gulf Coast: "Pantoum"

Indiana Review: "After she told me she was pregnant"

The Journal: "The Prodigies"

Literal Latté: "The Night Orchard"

The National Poetry Review: "New Dominion"

New England Review: "Olives, Bread, Honey, and Salt"

Nimrod: "Whitewater"

North American Review: "Our Campaign for Her World," "Robber girl," "Wind sonnet"

Seneca Review: "White Mushrooms"

The South Carolina Review: "Oil"

The Southern Review: "Ground Fire," "Trouble"

The Spoon River Poetry Review: "Barn Door," "Built it Ourselves, Out of Love and a Few Nails," "Dead heat," "(How to Fall from) Grace"

Terra Nova: "Vultures at Cold Canyon"

The title and italicized text in "Sparks, lights, and darkness" (part of "Eight questions") are from William Beebe's *Half Mile Down* (New York: Harcourt, Brace and Company, 1934).

"Wind sonnet" is composed of words for the wind in many different languages.

❧

I am very grateful to *The American Poetry Review*, the Honickman Foundation, and Copper Canyon Press. Much appreciation to Elizabeth Scanlon for shepherding this collection, and my deepest thanks to Mark Doty for his guidance, insight, and kindness.

For fellowships and awards that supported the writing of these poems, my gratitude to the Corporation of Yaddo, the Djerassi Foundation, the Dorothy Rosenberg Foundation, the Headlands Center for the Arts, the MacDowell Colony, the Montalvo Arts Center, the Ragdale Foundation, the Virginia Center for the Creative Arts, and the University of California at Davis—most especially Sandra McPherson, Sandra Gilbert, Gary Snyder, and Alan Williamson.

I am indebted to the members of the Thirteen Ways poetry group for providing a sense of community and for helping shape so many of these poems, and to Molly Peacock for showing me the way to the Juggernaut with such care and generosity.

I would like to thank Carol and Barry Stein, Debbi LaPorte, Major Jackson, Olivia Boler, Michelle Lovric, John Beckman, Ian Goldstein, John Poch, Pireeni Sundaralingam, Gregory Djanikian, Madeline Caum, and so many others who helped make this book possible. A warm thank you to Arielynn Cheng for use of the cover photograph.

A special thanks to Heather Stein for always being there; Robert Thomas for his tireless moral support and invaluable feedback on just about everything; Steve Shochet for so many years of friendship and comic relief; Brian Wood for truly understanding; and Kathy Rose, my home away from home. And of course to Steve Davy, for being there through rough and honey.